Reader Warning:

Bearennymies!

If you don't like my poems it's perfectly ok
Just be mindful late at night
For there are these awful, terrifying, high-flying,
Man-eating Bearennymies

Who just love to EAT my enemies!

LAUGHING
Poems for an Awesome! Life

School Spirit!

Some of the teachers at my school
Were in a mustache growing contest...

And all the men were trying to win it

However, the winner was Mrs. McGinnit..

Who didn't even know she was in it!

Hey Coach!

My Coach gave me an athletic cup
...I don't know what he was thinking

It's full of holes and smells real bad
...This cup is terrible for drinking!

T Wrecks

I know why the Tyrannosaurus Rex (T-Rex) are mad
I know why they seem so bad

They are supposed to be the world's meanest feeders
They are supposed to be the fearless-meat-eaters
They are supposed to be the grandest of the carnivores
There are supposed to be kings of the dinosaurs

The thing that drives them mad
The reason they are so bad
Is that they are sad :(

For all the power they should feel
One thing for sure is real
That with all the teeth and powerful legs, the killer tail
and the skin of scales
They only had 2 tiny little arms
And they could not seal the deal

They could not flex their biceps to show people they're cool
When they tried to high five, they looked like a fool

In an arm-wrestling contest
They'd never be best

Yes, even the fellow kangaroo tripod
Thought they were odd
Yes, they would give the T-Rex knocks
'cause "at least kangaroos can box"

No humor in their humerus for the poor T-Rex
After all, it can be lonely at the Apex

Pirate Chip!*

Arrrrrrr,
Did ya Sea Me pirate chip and Me pirate dip?
Ye Sea, Me can't have Me pirate chip without Me pirate dip!
That makes me one Irate Pirate!

Ya Sea, Me once ate Me pirate chip without Me pirate Dip
And the pirate chip, ya Sea, it broke off and flew into me
AYEEEEE!

It only be a second it took, ya Sea
For I forgot about Me hook, where Me hand used to be

So ya Sea, I be like a dead man, tellin' yee no lie
That's how I got this patch on Me AYEEEEE.

So, now that ya Sea
Allow Me ta spell 'Pirate' for yee:
P AYEEEEE aarrrrrrr aaaay T E

* For maximum
enjoyment I found
It's more fun to read this
with authentic pirate sounds!

Stalling

I have one question for you
A bit of a riddle:
Imagine you are in a public area
And you have to Poo, Pee or Piddle

Once in the restroom, you have to choose the right stall
Now, YOU can choose the ONE person
That walks out before you go in...
It's your call

So...Who would you want to walk out of the stall
Before you go 1, 2 or 3?

Well as for me,
It's The Restroom Stall Cleaner that I'd like to see!

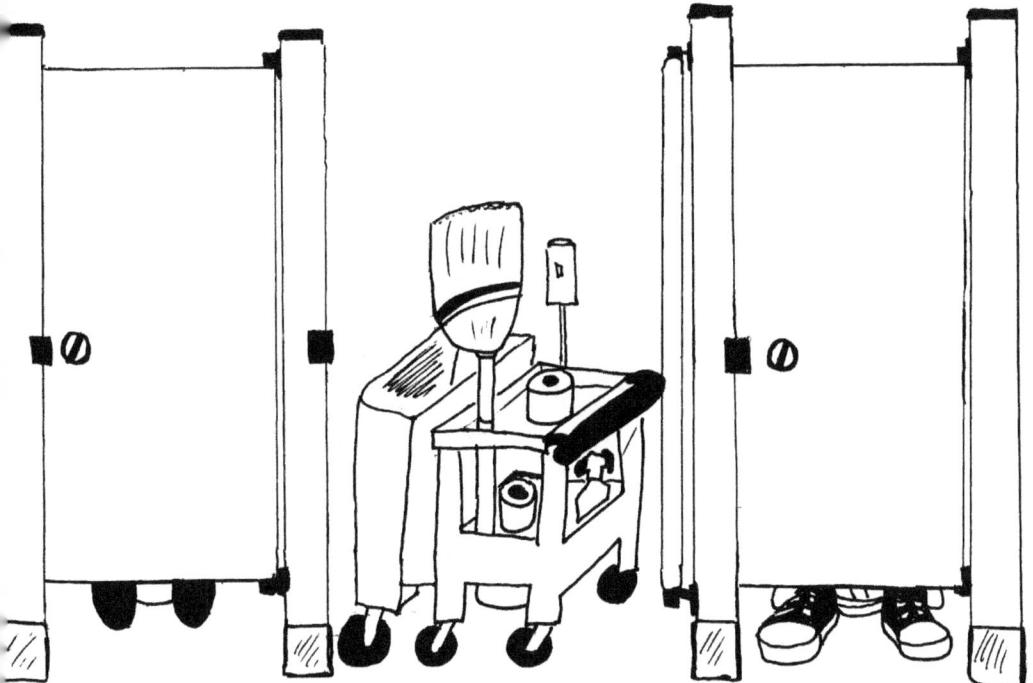

Monkey Tester

In our kitchen mom has lots of tools
Whisks and pots and pans and stools

Beaters and cups and spoons and bins
Waxed paper, aluminum foil and rolling pins

And THE most important thing in the room she says
"There is nothing better"
Then the ever-useful kitchen helper that she calls
the Monkey Tester

Spaghetti done Mom?
....."I need the Monkey Tester!"

Cake cooked Mom?
...."I need the Monkey Tester!"

Cookies ready Mom?
..."I need the Monkey Tester!"

Now, I don't know if the Monkey Tester is real...
She never let me see it.

'Cause whenever she needs one to test the food
I'm always there to eat it!

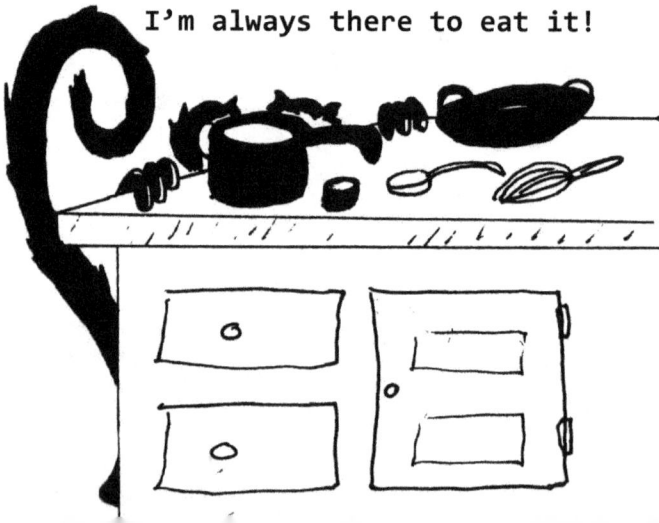

Lyin' Eyes

If you ever meet a person who doesn't like ice cream
Pizza, chocolate and apple pies

Please tell me
I'd like to meet them and look deep into their eyes

To see what else they are hiding
And why they tell such enormous lies

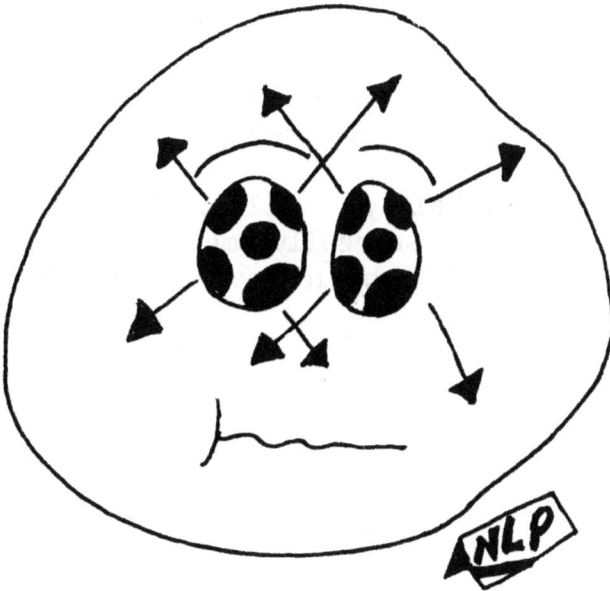

My Nose Knows

My nose smells
Sometimes it runs
Nevertheless, it always smells

Sometimes it smells Good
Sometimes it smells Bad
Sometimes it smells Trouble

However, it always smells...that's a fact
My nose really smells...
I wonder if I should have it looked at?

Naughty

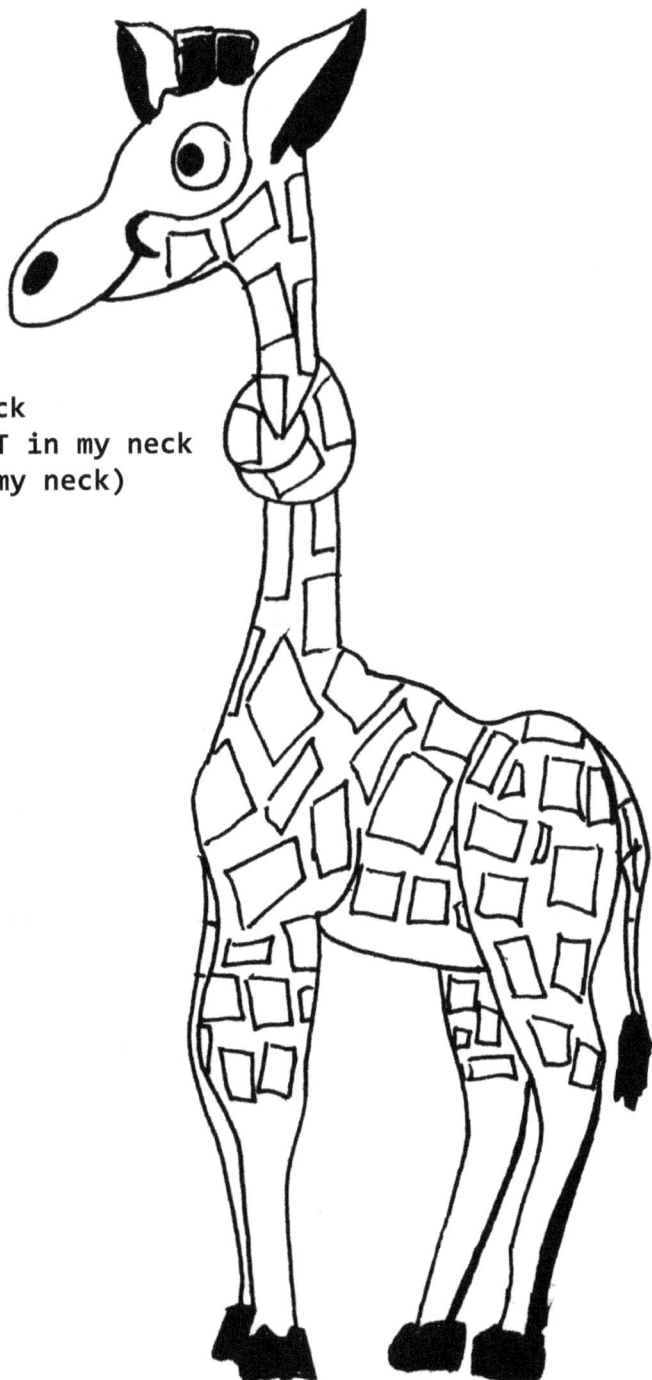

I have a KNOT in my neck
My doctor says it's NOT in my neck
(I think it's SNOT in my neck)

Faintin' Fanny

No one likes a Faintin' Fanny
Always sittin' when you need her

Getting' so tired of standin'
She has to relax and take a breather

Got some work to do..?
Faintin' Fanny takes a seat

Got to get somewhere in a hurry?
Faintin' Fanny rests a beat

Paintin'? Washin'? Cleanin'? Rakin'?
Faintin' Fanny takes a break

Scrubbin'? Movin'? Cookin'? Bakin'
It's downtime that Faintin' Fanny will be sure to take.

When I had a job to do with Dad
He would say 'Here comes Faintin' Fanny'

I heard so much about her -
I sat down and waited to greet her

She just never actually did show up
So I never got to meet her...

Elbows!

Abigail, Abigail strong and able,
Get your elbows off the table!

Emily, Emily strong and able,
Get your dollies off the table!!

Cade, Cade strong and able,
Get your books off the table!!!

Jackson, Jackson strong and able,
Get your tennis shoes off this table!!!

Marshall, Marshall strong and able,
Get your giant alligator off the....."Gulp"

Black Eye

I box 3 times a week
So I won't be meek

I wrestle in a club
So I won't look like a schlub

I practice Karate and Jujitsu
Taekwondo and Kung Fu

Nonetheless, how did I get my black eye?
To you......I must confess, I will not lie....

As I was putting on my headphones,
They slipped out of my hands like a rocket
And slammed into the side of my head
And bruised my left eye socket

Am I embarrassed? A little, I have to admit it
That's why I'll just tell people
It was a right hook that did it

And if they inquire more
About the black ring around my left eye
I will tell them
"Well, you should see the other guy!"

Running

What's with all the people who run?
Do they think it's so fun?
Are they running from someone?

They say it's a thrill
I say "it's not"
They say "let's go"
I say "let's stop"

POUNDING the pavement and HITTING the road
Sounds like a lot of pressure on my legs, knees and toes

I mean, when do you ever NEED to run?
I would rather relax in the midday sun

It's not like I'm in danger, so I just don't care
Running is overrated
It's not like I'm being chased by a B........!!!!!!!

Cockadoodle Don't

Allow me to present you "The World's Laziest Rooster"
His name is Cockadoodle Don't
When the other roosters wake early to greet the rising sun
He just won't

He sleeps all day long
Which I feel, just doesn't seem right
Because of all the time he spends
In the henhouse 'till late every night

The next poem is a poem of Poo
It's not, however a sweet story of Winnie the Poo
So, if that's what you are expecting
Then skip the next two pages
And go straight to 22!

365 Day Review

My plan is to write a unique book
...I know it's hard to do...
Especially when you hear what the subject is about
The book will be all about... Poo!

Yup, you heard me right
I've been thinking about it all night
To some the topic may be frightening
To me...The idea just hit me like lightning

So, here's how it will work, please try and follow
My plan is to start working on it first thing tomorrow

I will take the day off...
And eat only certain things
I will log them into a book
And then later examine the pay off

Yes, I will keep a log of....well... the logs
And then photograph the "end result"
A picture book of Poo's
It'll be reference book to consult

Yes, I will even make audio charts
To record each of the ......sounds

Yes, a history of the ins and the outs
Measuring the input and the output
The smallest one's a centimeter
The largest one's a foot!

It will require a lot of paperwork
And I certainly will be sitting a lot
I really don't care how much work it will be
I just don't give a squat!

There will be various chapters
On topics only seldom seen
I think I will have a special section
That's just focused on eating beans

The book will take 365 days to do
Yes...a 365 day review of Poo!

So, what do you think of a book all about Poo?
Would anyone buy it?
Would YOU?

Second Chance

O!
OH!
OH! NO!
My gum fell on the floor!
I can't chew it any more
Unless the 2 second rule applies
Oh, how the time flies!
My 2 seconds have elapsed!
My 2 second window has passed!
I can't enact it anymore!
So, there it remains on the floor!
Maybe I can extend the rule to '4'!
Yes, the rule can be adjusted for more!
I can now pick it up and chew
That was so easy to do
I don't like rules to be forsaken
On the other hand, sometimes, rules are made for breakin'

Miss Understood

"I have too Pee"
Says the boy at the ice cream stand
Mom drags him to the potty by the hand

"I have too Pee"
Says the boy at the flower store
Mom drags him to the loo's front door

"I have too Pee"
Says the boy at the ticket window
Mom drags him to the Restroom so he can 'go'.

Misunderstood!
Mom has no clue
He needs a new plan
He knows now what he can do!

"I'll have two please"
Writes the boy at the popcorn booth
Amazing how different things can sound
When you're missing your front tooth.

Who's Training Who?

He barks for his food
He's borderline rude
He stands at the door for attention

He demands food scraps
He takes long daily naps
And he licks himself in places too awkward to mention

He whines to go outside
He asks to go for car rides
"Roll down the windows" he likes the air in his face

"Bring me Here" he growls
"Bring me There" he howls
He pulls and drags us from place to place

Our dog doesn't think it's nice
That he always has to ask more than twice
For us to understand just what he desires

He must think we are fools
He's looking into owner's obedience schools
So he can get just what he requires

Napkin Please!

Of all the things
There's never been
Something so strangely unused
As a kid's napkin

Children seldom use the napkins you lay on their lap
Nor the ones you drape to protect their skirt
They always prefer the napkins
That are attached to the arms of their shirts!

Yes, the sleeves, that what the kids use
That's the wiping device they never refuse
It's built in, handy and works just great
So, there's no reason to use
The napkin by their plate

Yes, why do grown-ups bother placing a napkin on the table?
When a kid's shirt sleeve is so willing and able

To wipe their mouths "We'll use our sleeves" the kids say
To them, there's nothing better
Unless, you are nearby to them when they are eating
And then they prefer to use the sleeves
Of your brand-new sweater

Ouch!

While sitting under the coconut tree
A BIG idea suddenly crossed my brain...
That there are much better places to take a break
That aren't nearly so full of pain

Scared Straight

I had been noticing that my hair always looks the best
On the day of my haircut, it's always so well-tressed

How does it know? Does it talk to the scissors?
Is my hair aware of the clippers?

To me, my hair seems unwilling to be:

Arched & Banged
Tapered And Blocked

Crowned & Parted
Layered and Cropped

Dusted & Blunted
Brushed and Shaved

Busted & Razored
Dyed and Waved

Glossed & Colored
Tossed and Glazed

Do the scissors scare my hair in place?
Now, I pretend to make an appointment everyday...
To save myself the hassle and waste

Yes, my hair is always ready in a minute
On the days it thinks there's a haircut in it

Music Lessons

Can I ask you a question?
The answer you may know it
My grandfather gave me this shoe-horn
Do you know how I'm supposed to blow it?

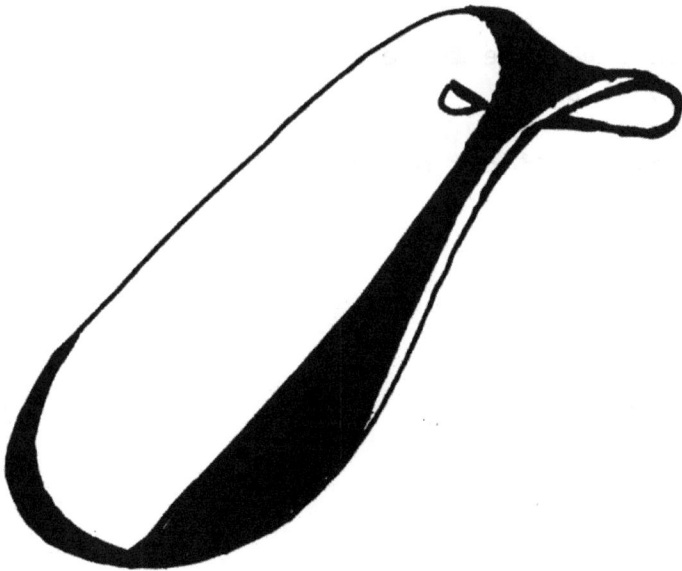

Your "But"

Please
Please!
I'm on my knees

Begging
Pleading
This is what I'm really needing!

I've told you once
I've told you two times or even three
When you say something nice to me…

And you don't want me to Pout:(at it
Or even SHOUT! at it
Please, please!
Keep your big 'BUT' out of it

Grrrrrr

I played a tiger
In the school play last night,
There's just one thing
That doesn't seem quite right:

I wanted to be as natural,
And authentic as a tiger can be
I didn't wear any costume,
I only painted tiger stripes on me
So, why then did everyone laugh
At the sight of me?

Shall I turn around,
So you can see?

Magic Snow

My older brother and his friends
Let me in on a secret
He made me swear that I would keep it

One night,
The snow was deep and wintery white
They took me to show me the secret
We walked all night
Under the moonlight
Until, we finally reached it

We came to a place where the snow was not just white...
And not just cold
This snow was the color of GOLD!

That's right, the 'Magic Snow'
Right before my eyes!
So, I asked him what made this snow so tricky
He told me this magic snow is full of hot leprechaun gold
And that's what makes it so sticky

He told me that when I touched the golden snow to my lips
Everyone will drop their defenses
And lose control of their senses
And I will be the center of attention
And I will turn the room into a laughing convention

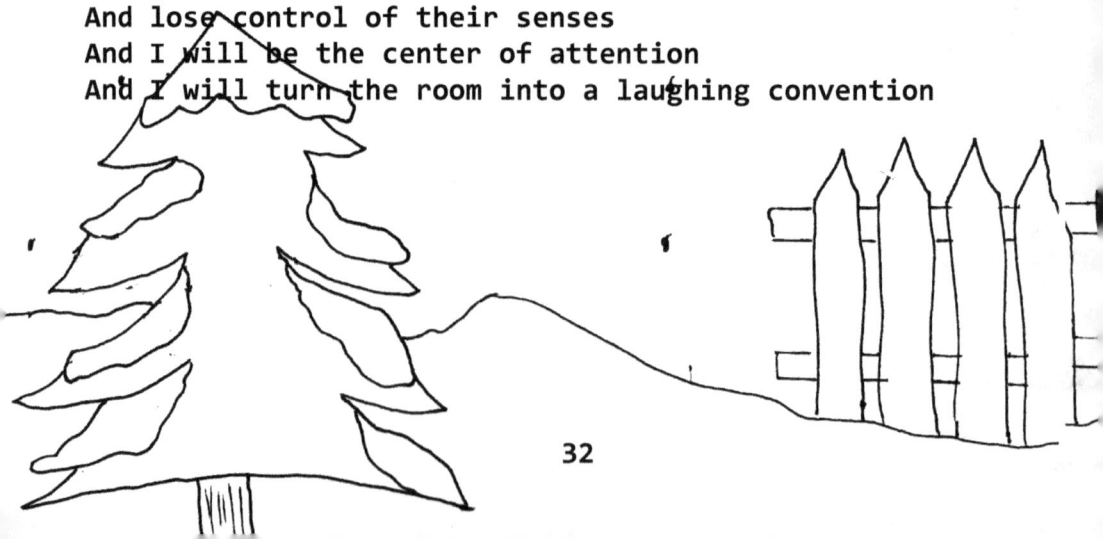

To be able to wield so much power
To create such a true happy hour
By only eating the Golden snow
It seemed like a big win
To be the cause of many chuckles and grins
So, I decided it was the only way to go

Yes, my brother and his friends screamed with pleasure
As I was unafraid to taste the Golden treasure
And they enjoyed it immensely for over an hour
Only later the next day did my glee go away
When the taste in my mouth turned sour

That's when I saw my neighbor's dog behind a tree
Lifting his leg to take a p...

Well let's just say he made more "golden snow"

Yes, that special "Golden Snow" made my brother's friends
Burst with laughter
I never knew 'til the moment I saw the dog, just exactly
What they were after

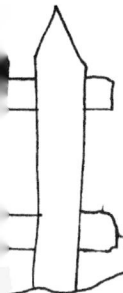

Dessert Belly

That boy has two stomachs!
Please don't ask me how
He has a segmented gut
Kinda just like a cow

When he's eating a meal...
He'll tell you "I'm full"
He puts down his fork...
And jumps right off his stool

You want to bring him back to the table?
Tell him there's a dessert you've been makin'
Because even if his Dinner Belly's full
He has room in his Dessert Belly that always seems vacant

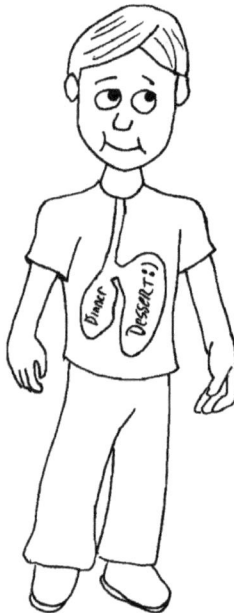

Aye To Pie!

Pie is better than Cake!
That's a statement I feel I must make

You see, Pie is made to be yummy
To feel cozy in your tummy

The thing about Cake that I'm-seeing
Is it's less about the cake and more about the icing

Why, it can take up to 700 steps to bake a Cake
A Pie is so much easier to make

Cake is made to be ornate
Cake's main purpose is to decorate
Adorned with Toppers and lace and piping with a border
With dragees? And pearls and pillars made to order

This is simply not the case for Pie
For Pie is made to be eaten
And that is why it can't be beaten

So, next time you want to bake a Cake to celebrate
Please consider, the obvious alternate
It's round, it's flaky and pleasing to the eye
Friends, I'm talking about a nice wholesome Pie

My preference for Pie
Please keep just to yourself, please don't repeat it
Because, if someone offers me some Cake
I'm probably gonna eat it

My Beard

It seems that no one likes my beard
Everyone says that my beard is weird

Everyone tells me that all through the day
Everyone yells at me to shave it away

The man at the store
Says my beard is a bore

And just yesterday, a woman came up to me, strangely enough
Handed me a few coins and asked me "How did times get so tough?"

Even kids make me feel like a total disgrace
When they see me they cry "Here comes old hairy face"

The fact that my dogs keep barking at me, is wearing me thin
I assume they think I have 24 cats hanging on my chin

However, I think if I decided to shave it off today
No one would have anything to say

So, by keeping my beard growing
At least it's me they'll be knowing

And besides, if I shave off my beard
Then everyone will find out
What I've been so hesitant to disclose:
Shhh, can you keep a secret?....
I don't own any clothes!

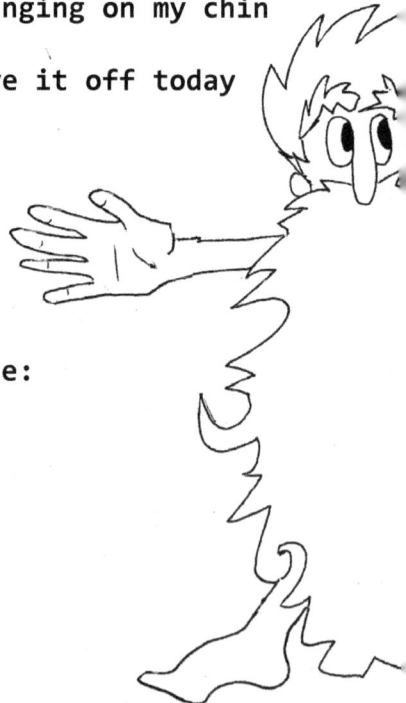

What A P.I.T.A.!

I went to the doctor today and in detail I explained
That every time I sit, I have a severe and sharp pain

And that the pain is so excruciating
It's giving me quite a scare

The receptionist nodded her head,
Handed me a number and said

"Please have a seat over there"

Slurpin' Sherman

Slurpin' Sherman's Dad's not proud
'cause Slurpin' Sherman eats too loud!

Slurpin' Sherman's Mom's aghast
'cause Slurpin' Sherman eats too fast!

Stay far away from Slurpin' Sherman
When he's enjoying his soup du jour
And be nowhere near Slurpin' Sherman
When he's eating' watermelon
For listening to that noise is just pure torture!

Slurpin' Sherman doesn't mean to be rude
He's only trying to eat his food

Yes, Slurpin' Sherman wants to finish the food on his plate
-He doesn't want to waste it
Slurpin' Sherman should slow down a bit when he's eating
-Maybe then he would taste it

No Floss, No Fuss

I'm a figuring that flossing my teeth is
  something I'll not be a needin'

I tried it once, a while back,
and my gums were all a bleedin'

Brainfreeze!

Oh MY! I drank this frozen slushie too fast!
OOOW! HOW long is this pain gonna last?
YIKES! ICE is coursing through my veins
It feels like an icicle is jabbing at my brain!

PHEW, YOU know the pain is now going away
I thought that headache would ruin this sunny day!
Yes, the torture is now receding
So, a hospital stay I'll no longer be needing

WOW, HOW that was ever a bad trip!
Now I'm FINE, TIME for the second sip....

Where Are You?

The doctor gave me a prescription for the pain in my rear
He said take "2 pills and your pain will disappear"
After I took them, I looked for you, I swear!
I just couldn't find you anywhere!

The Itsnot Fair

I went to the Itsnot Fair
I met the strangest salesman there
He had no customers in his tent
I wondered where they all went

I went inside to peek around
He hadn't any merchandise to be found
So, I asked him what he was selling
Otherwise, I had no way of telling

"It-Snot for sale" he mentioned
"It's Not for sale?" I questioned
"That's right" he replied
"From the right and the left side"

"What's not for sale?" I inquired
"It-Snot!" He fired
"I don't get it" I retorted
"That's why I'm selling it" He snorted

"Selling what?!" I began yelling
He shouted "It-Snot that I'm selling!"

42

"I don't see any here!" I bested
He told me "It's made fresh when requested'
I told him "You have nothing in your store!"
He told me "When I need some, I make more"

"More of what?" I demanded
"It-Snot that I sell" he commanded

I inquired "Then what do you do to make money?"
(My nose was starting to get runny)
"I sell!" he stated with a smile, trying to be funny

"Sell what!?!" I started to cry
"And now you made me all teary-eyed!"
I asked "Do you have a tissue I can use?"
He gave me one looking amused

I blew my nose loudly,
And he said "You're welcome" very proudly
He jibed "That'll be two-seventy five"
And he held out his hand to retrieve it
"You're charging me for a napkin?" I couldn't believe it!

"No, It-Snot is what-sfor sale" he explained again to me,
"For you today, The tissues... are free"
Exhausted, I said "I only have a 50 cents and a dollar"
I expected him to rant and holler
He complied "That's fine, no trouble"
"Tomorrow you can pay me double"

I ran out of the tent confused,
So, don't let me go back there! Please you must remind me!
"It-Snot for sale!"
I heard him telling new customers behind me

Peepee Dance

Look at that boy watching the movie over there...
The one that can't sit still in his chair!
He's wiggling his seat...
And shuffling his feet!

His hands are all fisted...
His lips are all twisted!

He's sweating, He's shaking...
His legs are all quaking!

That boy needs to leave, he just won't take the chance!
That boy is doing the Peepee dance!

That boy is enjoying the movie so much,
He doesn't want to be missin' it...
If he doesn't go to the bathroom soon,
His chair is gonna have pissin' it !

Ill-Mannered Mike

Ill-Mannered Mike
Loves to talk to his food
Even though his parents, teachers and friends
Tell him it's super-duper rude

"See ya later" he forewarns the corn
"Smell ya later" he discusses with the asparaguses
"Hear ya later" he screams to the beans
"Feel ya later" he tosses to the hot sauces

According to him:
"Food should not be wasted,
...By only being tasted"

According to him:
"You should only eat the foods that are 'so nice',
...That you get to 'enjoy them twice'"

I don't know if Ill-Mannered Mike is
Right or wrong
Or
A saint or a sinner

I don't know if Ill-Mannered Mike is
A real rude dude
Or
If he's growing fat or even shrinking thinner

I just laugh every time
That I listen to him eat his dinner

Sharin' Meels

Sharin Tings married Mr. Meels
And everything went well at first
However, Sharin Tings got heavy
And Mister Meels got light
Because Sharin Tings ate double her share
You see, Mr. Meels … was way too polite

Beware The Leaner

In all the world, there's absolutely no one meaner
Then the inconsiderate and hideous "dinner-table leaner"

They may look perfectly innocent that's true
When they pretend to stretch their back...just to fool you

While you eat
They "adjust their seat"
While you chew
They "Bend askew"

However, there is a reason
For this little dance
And it's not because
They are "fixing their pants"

So, next time you sit
Next to someone of low class
And they start to lean
Shifting their center of mass
Beware, It's not the ketchup
They're about to pass

Two-Short

"You must be this tall to ride this ride"
Said the sign in front of the long line outside

Yes, our "gang" was at the amusement park
I was there alone, with all my crew
We were all waiting in line for you

There was "High-Haired Harry"
And "Wide-Browed Barry"
"Fore-Headed Freddie"
And "Long-Legged Betty"

"Snake-Eared Susie"
And "Double-Chinned Dewey"
"Pencil-Necked Nick"
And "Thick-Heeled Rick"

Harry's brother "Mike"
Why, even your pal "Spike!"

And me, "Cowboy Billy"
(My new nickname made me feel a little silly)
Because I was wearing cowboy boots and my 10 gallon hat
I didn't want anyone making fun of me
For looking like that!

Except for the fact that you weren't there
In the end the trip was a success
We all REALLY missed you... "2-Inch Tess"!

One Keen Machine

I have an idea for a new machine
I will sell them in red, orange, yellow and green
You will never again have to do housework or clean
For all your chores will be done for you faster than a
Cheetah high on caffeine

This machine will put away your clothes
It will floss your teeth nightly
It will empty the dish washer
It will answer your phone politely

This machine will keep your room tidy
It will tie your loose laces
It will keep your bookshelf neat
It will pick food from your braces

This machine will carry your books to school
And take all your tests
It will do whatever needs to be done
And anything else you request

So, now all I have to do is just start creatin' it
The world needs this machine, there's just no debatin' it!
I'm starting on a plan now, it may take me a few days
Or maybe a year
And where to begin, well...I'm not exactly clear

In the meantime,
I'll just keep using my little brother
(Please don't tell my mother)

The Truth About The Tooth

I caught my Dad trying to steal my TOOTH last night!
This really bothers me, this just isn't right!

I've been growing that tooth for nearly 10 years
Yesterday it fell out, and I put it under my stuffed bunny
(Mr Long Ears)

I was deep asleep when I felt something
Rustling my tooth under my rabbit
I opened my eyes and saw MY Dad trying to grab it!

My Dad looked surprised and scared
Man, this is really starting to bug me!
When my Mom heard me screaming, she came right in to hug me

I can't believe my own Father would steal my tooth!
Maybe for the money...
Strange though, because when I caught him
He already had 5 dollars in his other hand!
No, this just isn't funny!

Wait until my Grandparents find out
About his attempt to steal my tooth!
He'll have to face the whole family
And confess the real truth!

The fact that my Dad tried to steal my tooth
Is disturbingly scary!
I just can't figure out why anyone else would want my tooth
Besides of course, me and the tooth fairy

Wiggly Jiggly Tooth

Wiggle Wiggle
Jiggle Jiggle
My tooth is coming loose!

Side to side
Backward forward
It's freeing from its roots!

It tickles me, it itches me and now it kinda hurts
The feeling is so uniquely weird
That I think I'm about to burst!

The last time that I lost a tooth
I remember the feeling was kind of fun
The hole seemed HUGE when I felt it with my tongue
Although, my finger felt a much smaller one

Right now my Wiggly Jiggly tooth is still in
So for now I must mind it
I just hope when it eventually falls out
The tooth fairy can help me find it

And if losing this tooth negatively affects
My beautiful smiling grin
I always have the option to stick it right back in!

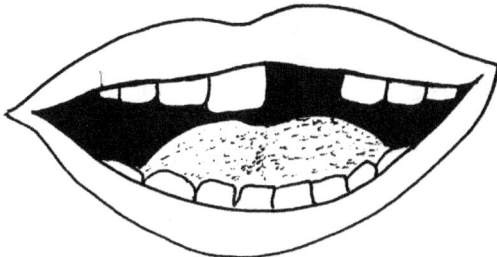

Hold The Mold

For most people, when they see mold growing on cheese,
It's REALLY not so nice.

'cept the French grocers,
When they see green on the cheese,
They just 'Jacque-up' the price!

Periodic Pun

The 'Periodic Table of the Elements" states:
The symbol for Plutonium is "PU"
I think as far as planetary minerals go,
"PU" would better describe Uranus…
Don't U?

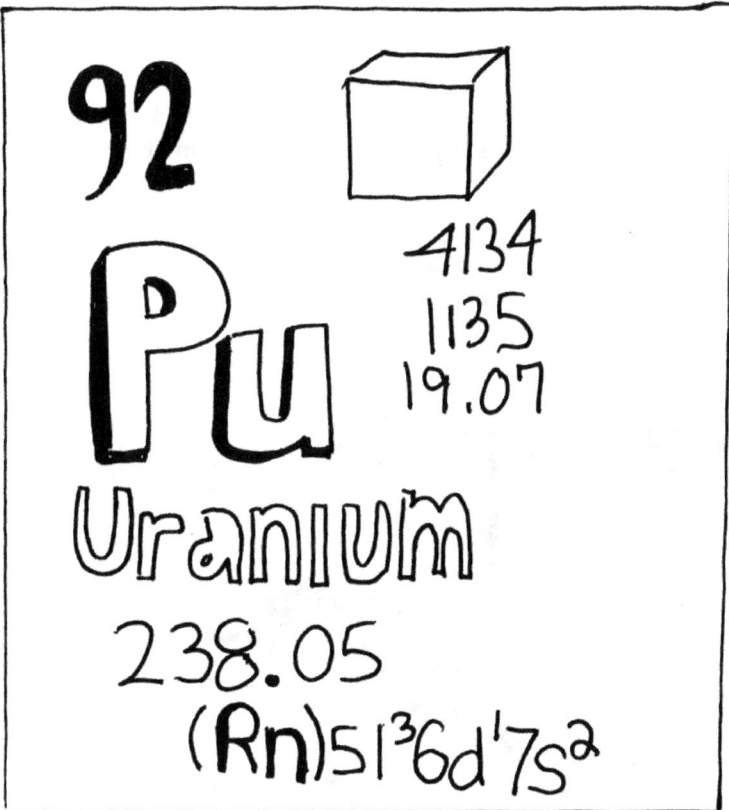

92

Pu

4134
1135
19.07

Uranium

238.05

(Rn)5f³6d¹7s²

Explosion!

My little boy must have exploded!
I can't find him anywhere!

All I see are his shirt, his socks,
His shoes, his shorts and his underwear!

Scattered Everywhere!

My little boy must have exploded
I really can't explain it any more...

Because, I've already told him a million times
Not to leave his clothes lying on the floor!

Whatta Downer!

I feel so bad for the poor old widow Ms. Van Zown!
She lived with her 7 sons in a little cottage
At the head of town…
And throughout the years
Not one of her boys EVER put the toilet seat down!

Peephole People

The people in my peephole are always so contorted
Their faces are stretched to the maximum
And their features are all distorted!

I'm glad I can see the people through my peephole
And one day I want to thank the inventor
Because all the visitors to my front door
Are so strange looking!
I sure don't want them to enter!

Musee"uhm"

Went to the 'Museum of the Most Modern Art' today
So, ahh, what can I say?

I saw a pile of rubbish on the ground
I saw splashes on the wall
I saw too much of some things
And of others, nothing at all

I saw workers preparing an exhibit
The area filled with people gaping in mid-stare
As the corded-cooling work fan hanging from the ceiling
Was revolving and spinning in mid-air

I saw an elephant rolling on the floor
I saw a Dutch masterpiece costing billions
I was annoyingly infatuated by a video of a woman screaming
And I saw evidence of human brilliance

So, I was entertained and dazzled
And I was bewildered and frazzled
It changed my perception about what I believe
And inspired my reception of what the mind can conceive

It's just that... with some modern art pieces
I wonder what a few accomplished artists were thinking
Because some of the art they have created
Only accomplished art that is stinking

If I Had A Zoo...

My teacher Ms. Magoo
Just gave us an annoying writing project to do
The assignment is called "If I had a Zoo..."
How to start this? I just don't have a clue!
Well, I don't know about you
I do know one thing is true:
If I did have a Zoo
The first one I'd put in a cage is old "you know who"
(That would be Ms. Magoo)
(Let's just keep that between Me and You)

Common Cents

Hey U!
Do you want to hear a secret?
If I tell you, will you promise me that you'll keep it?

My Mom thinks that I am a perfect angel
And that I never do any wrong
If she hears about this
She may be singing a different song!

Well, here it is: >>> (between me and you)
Do you know how, when you wash your hair…?
That the amount of shampoo you are supposed
To use should be about the size of a dime?
And they write that on every shampoo bottle, all the time?

Well, (don't tell my Mom)…
Shhh…here's the secret …..I use much more than I Oughta!
I use about the size of a Quarta'!

Hair Today

I think by now my body should be knowing
To stop producing all the hair
In the places I don't want it growing

No matter what I do to the hair
It always comes back, to my despair

On top of my toes
And inside of my nose

Under my armpits
I just can't seem to stop it

All over my legs and below my Hip
And I can never get rid of the mustache
Appearing daily on my lip

Small ones pop out randomly on my shoulder, back and rear
And today my best friend pulled a big one
Right out of my ear!

And there seems to be no way to win this race
Of keeping all this hair from growing all over my face
As soon as I shave it off and turn
From the mirror near the sink
It starts to grow back, faster than you'd ever think!

It's no use, fighting the never-ending battle with this hair
I just wish it would grow thicker on my...
Well, you know where...

Losing It

Mom said that YOU said you would be home an hour ago,
That's what YOU told her,
Mom said that you are getting more and more forgetful,
As you get older,
Mom said that your head sometimes seems,
As hard as a boulder,
Mom said that you'd lose your head,
If it wasn't attached to your shoulders!

Uncle Bob's Tighty Whiteys

Uncle Bob's Tighty Whiteys ain't too tight
Uncle Bob's Tighty Whiteys ain't too white

Uncle Bob tries to get his Tighty Whiteys
Brighter than bright
Uncle Bob bleaches and scrubs his Tighty Whiteys
With all his might

After washin' 'em, Uncle Bob hangs
His Tighty Whiteys outside to dry at night
Under the moonlight
There's just something about Uncle Bob's Tighty Whiteys
That just ain't right

All our neighbors complain that Uncle Bob's Tighty Whiteys
Give them a fright
I don't mean to be uptight, it's just that Uncle Bob needs
To keep them Tighty Whiteys out of our sight!

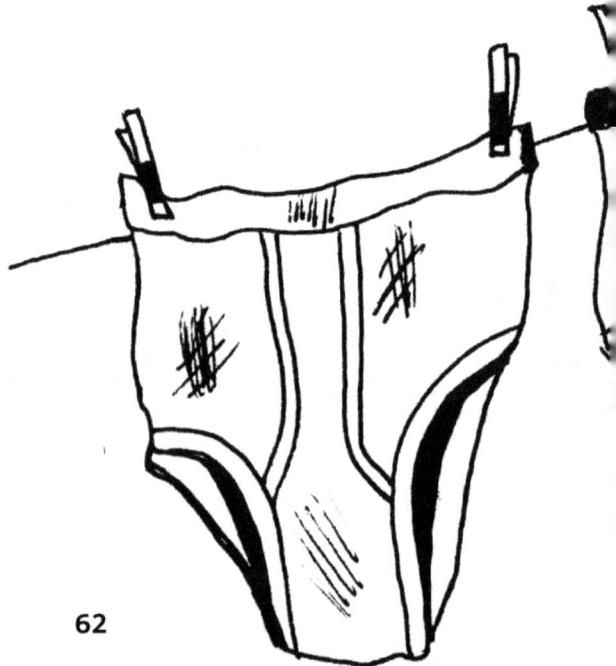

Waste-Band Of Brothers

Something was making me super-cranky
I was just not feeling right
There was a strange feeling in my gut
It was bothering me all night

Then I realized, what was amiss
And why I was in such despair
I was wearing someone else's underwear!

And the fact they weren't mine
Didn't really bother me at all
It's just they were no less than three sizes too small!

Go Or No-Go Decision

Toilet flushing can account for 25 percent
Of a household's water use
The talking heads say that 'peeing while showering'*
May cut down on this abuse!

It's sterile, and non-toxic
And may cure athlete's foot infections
You just have to be sure you aim in the right directions!

Sure, the topic may be sensitive
So, we have to take the matter in our own hands
Friends, neighbors, and eco-people
It's time to make a stand!

So, the next time you wash up and you find yourself alone
Please remember
Only pee in the shower if you are bathing in your own home!

*(Although peeing in the shower may be
An environmentally friendly thing to do
Do not under any circumstance take a bath in the loo!)

Fill 'er Up!

I'm so full of this food!
I may have eaten too much of it!
I'm so full of this food, I'm sure I can almost touch it!

The food is up to my throat
And it's beginning to linger
I think I can feel it with the tip of my finger!

Yep, I can touch it. There I just did!
And now the food's starting to go up!
Oh no! I think I'm going to throw up!

Chipmunk Shipping

How much cheap chip can a chipmunk cheaply ship
If a chipmunk could cheaply ship chip?

Big Bold Bobbie Bray

Big Bold Bobbie Bray woke up one sunny day,
He stretched his arms and went to the toilet to pee
Big Bold Bobbie Bray passed a mirror along the way,
So, he paused a second to see what he could see.

Big Bold Bobbie Bray was more than surprised,
You might say,
When he saw hands growing from
Where his nipples used to be!

Big Bold Bobbie Bray started screaming "HIP HIP HOORAY!",
When he realized his wish had become a reality.

Big Bold Bobbie Bray
Dropped to his knees and began to pray,
He thanked the Lord for the blessings bestowed on he.
For Big Bold Bobbie Bray
Had to clean his bedroom that very day,
So, he wished for a set of helping hands to make it easy.

Big Bold Bobbie Bray
Finished in short-time cleaning his room that day,
However, his nipple-hands were hardly used at all, sadly.
Big Bold Bobbie Bray
Soon wished these new hands would go away,
And it seemed this wish after all turned out quite badly

Though they stayed put for life on his chest rather steady
Big Bold Bobbie Bray soon realized along the way,
At the ends of his arms already
Were all the helping hands he ever needed to display

The Hunt

I'm on a hunt for a dangerous Asian one-horned rhino today
If you happen to see one around
Please let me know, right away!

What's The Reel Line?

Dad took us fishing
We cast the lines
Over 200 times!
Without getting the lines tangled
Or mangled!
And we all thought it was great!
Dad?… Well, he says he only counted 8!

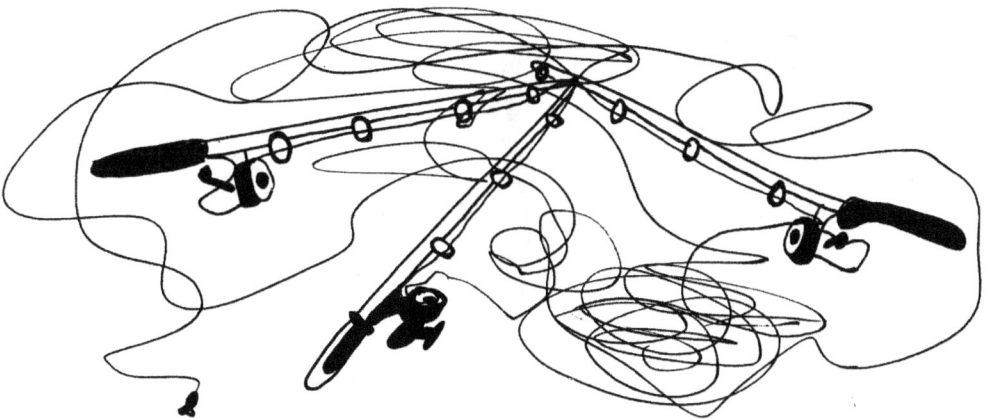

When To Say "When"

When you are eating a meal
And you're almost finished
Please Stop just before you start licking the plate
And rubbing your tummy
(Unless of course there's no one around,
And it tastes really yummy!)

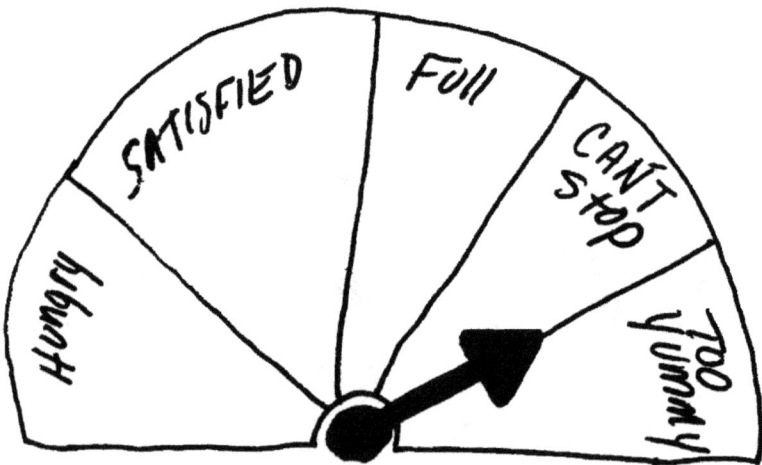

Monster Under My Refrigerator

There's a scary Monster that lives under my refrigerator
He eats the bits of food that happen to fall on the floor

You must be very careful of his long-long fingernails
'Cause he can reach to the second shelf on the door

He must need the light from the fridge to live
For when the door is open he grows and glows!

And especially watch out, late at night
When your belly needs a snack
'Cause what he really loves to eat is TOES!

Playing With Your Food

There's nothing like smellin'...
A fresh Watermelon

I like to play scrabble...
While munching and crunching an Apple

While talking with Anna...
I always eat a Banana

I prefer to read stories that are scary...
As I nibble Cherries and Berries

And it only seems fair...
To share a nice juicy Pear

I just can't find anything...
ANYTHING
Interesting to do with an Orange!

The Dance

Girls on the left
Boys on the right
The music surrounds them
However, no dancing yet tonight

The girls look pretty
The boys look smooth
Yet, no one seems to make a move

For hours and hours
Only wallflowers

With snickers, looks and giggles
The dance has not yet produced a wiggle

Girls on the left
Boys on the right

This dance is tremendous
Oh, what a night!

Orange, you
needed on
page 72?

Hurtin' For Certain

I tried all the home cures
For a bad stomach ache
Sipping tea with honey and ginger
Mixed with the hottest chocolate I can make

Eating peppermint, pasta and applesauce
Oatmeal, yogurt, rice and a salad freshly-tossed
Sprinkled with Cherries, Raisins, Prunes and Apricots

I tried Heating it and cooling it...at the same time...
No lies
Then I went outside for some exercise
Cartwheels, front flips
Hanging upside down and deep dips

Now my stomach is really killing me
Next time, before I try the cures...
I will wait until my stomach is actually illing me

Suzy Sunshine

Eat your granola Suzy Sunshine
Don't pay my food any mind
You like the foods you like
And I like mine just fine!

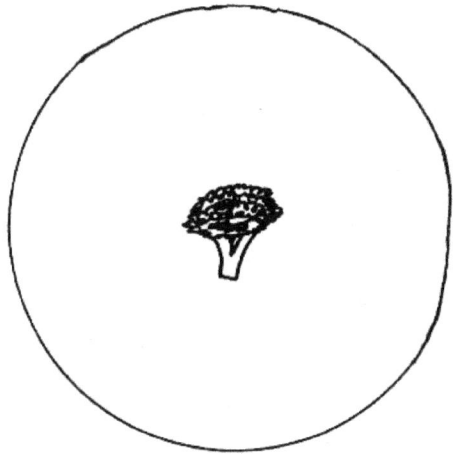

Toenail Soup

As I was growing up
My toenails grew longer and longer
And I could always tell when it was time to clip them
As the odor from my shoes kept getting
Stronger and stronger

So, I would sit in my quiet place to clip them
Right on the front door stoop
When Mom heard me trimming my toenails
She'd yell "Save them for Toenail Soup!"

So, I've been saving up my toenails
In a jar, right under my bed
For my entire life, doing just what my Mom had said

To save time, I was told "You can add fingernails too"
"However, they will dilute the soup"
"Toenails are more tasty!"
So, Mom warned me "Don't be so hasty!"

I never knew if it was in jest
I just figured that Mom always knew best

And although I never saw her make a pot of it
I kind of always wanted to taste it, not eat a lot of it

So the other day, I finally made it
Yes, I made a batch of Toenail Soup!
The broth, the stock, the whole shebang!
So, I will let you in on the scoop

All my life, in my Mother I've been trusting
I have to tell you the honest truth
"That soup is disgusting!"

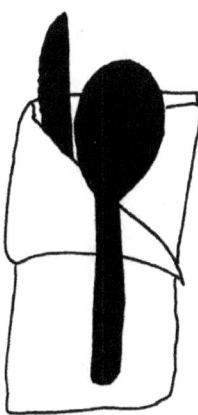

About the Author

J. Leone is the author-artist of the 3 part series Living, Laughing and Loving, Poems for an Awesome! Life.

He is a private business owner, a writer of songs and available for public speaking.

He can be spotted in Awesome! places like New York City; Princeton, NJ; Miami, FL; Amsterdam, The Netherlands and on the beautiful Caribbean island of St. Maarten.

GreenSpring
greenspringnv@gmail.com